500+ AFFIRMATIONS FOR BLACK KIDS

Empower Them with Gratitude, Build
Their Confidence, Help to Inspire,
Increase Motivation, Positivity, Success,
Healing, Self-Love and Self-Esteem

Rashinique Farrell

TABLE OF CONTENTS

INTRODUCTION

I remember waiting for my turn to use the slide in the park when I was six. They were four of us waiting, and one older girl with pretty blonde hair muttered sweetly, *"Let the black girl go first."* I was left confused for a few seconds, thinking about which one of us was the black girl. Then, everyone started looking at me with expectations that I go down the slide, and at that moment, I realized I was the *black girl.*

I was never aware of what **race** was until that point in my life. Despite being best friends with a white girl then, I never noticed our physical differences. After the slide experience, I went home with many questions for my parents. I tried convincing them that my skin was brown and not black, so *"why should anyone refer to me as black?"*

My parents knew that day would eventually come; the day my race would be pointed out to me. Thankfully, my parents were prepared for that day. They sit me down to discuss my roots and why I am different from others. They made me feel comfortable and reminded me to always be my authentic self and be comfortable in my skin.

However, I soon tasted the other side of being black. In middle school, other kids started laughing at me for being *black.* They were segregations and preferential treatment given to the white folks; even the teachers weren't left out. I was bullied and picked on every single day.

I liked wearing my natural hair in an Afro, and my classmates would laugh at me and ask why my hair wasn't straightened.

The questions and unfair treatment got to me and made me feel different from everyone else. A teacher once told me my hair was a distraction and made my mum pick me up from school.

It's not just me; institutional racism affects children in K-12 schools. Research studies, anecdotes from families, and many discrimination lawsuits reveal that black kids are discriminated against in schools. They are less likely to be recognized for their greatness, disciplined more harshly, and not treated equally with other kids. Today many black kids have been bombarded with negative images of themselves.

This is a rude awakening for black parents. While they try their best to protect their kids from what may hurt them, they must provide them with the tools that will help them overcome any adversity.

I was able to get through the hate I was faced with and navigate through a difficult childhood with the affirmations my parents taught me. Affirmations reminded me of my importance in the world; they reinforced my values and confirmed that I was never alone. They assisted me by building my self-confidence, awareness, self-love, and self-acceptance.

Teaching kids to love themselves can be the difference between success and failure in the long run. Reciting affirmations can add value to kids' lives and those surrounding them. As someone that has witnessed the power of affirmations first-hand, I know the importance of repeating them and their impact on one's mental health.

Even though we can't control how people view us, we can shape how we view ourselves. We can use affirmations to frame our identity positively despite the negative and dangerous narrative from the broader society.

Affirmations for black kids are important. Every day, black kids hear that they aren't good enough; they are told they are lesser beings through stereotypes and prejudice. The media refers to them as the sidekick. Advertisers and children's toy companies made it seem black kids have limited options and lack access to representation.

Black kids need to start using affirmations as early as they can to make it easier to build an optimistic worldview.

Reciting affirmations every morning will breathe life into the lives of black kids, helping them start a new day with positivity. Our words carry so much power, and when young, innocent minds use their words positively, it's even more powerful.

This book contains 500 best affirmations for black kids to incorporate into their daily lives. The positive and encouraging words in this book will help lift black kids and shape their self-worth.

Affirmations only require a few seconds to make a huge difference in a kid's life.

Now let's start affirming!

CHAPTER ONE: AFFIRMATIONS FOR SELF-LOVE AND HAPPINESS

1. I see myself and my abilities; I am unique in so many ways.
2. I have great value.
3. I am alive and here for a reason.
4. I love all my flaws.
5. I don't need to be perfect to be loved.
6. I am proud of who I am.
7. There is no one better than me.
8. No one else is like me in the world; I am unique.
9. I lack perfection, but I love everything about myself.
10. I love my color, hair, skin, and body.
11. I am beautiful and lovable.
12. I am appreciated and proud of who I am becoming.
13. I am a black kid with a positive body image.
14. I will only use kind words for myself.
15. I am loved by my parents and everyone around me.
16. I find love in what is inside me and not what is outside.
17. I am uniquely made, and I was made for a reason.
18. I am comfortable in my skin, and I absolutely love it.
19. I am filled with happiness, love, and joy.

20. I am worthy of my love, and I won't stop feeding myself with love.
21. Loving myself gives me happiness.
22. I feel and look awesome.
23. I am open to everything good.
24. I am valuable; my treasures are within me.
25. I am thankful for who I am.
26. Receiving love from others starts with loving myself, and I love myself.
27. I love who I am and will continue rewarding myself with positive thoughts.
28. I will always make myself the best.
29. I am open to seeing my beauty and my grandness.
30. I always choose happiness regardless of how my happiness makes others feel.
31. I am enough for myself.
32. I am the real deal; the premium package.
33. I can't blame others for how they feel about me. If they hate me, it's their loss.
34. I won't give anyone the key to my happiness.
35. It's a new dawn of greatness; I am determined to stay happy and loved.
36. I am blessed to experience real love from my parents.
37. Every day, I will unravel new ways of loving myself.
38. I am gentle and patient with myself. It reflects on those around me.
39. My self-love boosts the capacity of love I have for others.
40. I create positive vibes around people.
41. I am working to be my best version.
42. I fit into anywhere I walk; I don't need to squeeze in to earn my worth.
43. I deserve the beautiful relationships I have with my parents, family, and friends.
44. I am black, and my color speaks for itself.
45. I will always stay true to myself; that's how I win.

46. I am happy with all the love I have in my life.
47. I will focus my energy on what gives me love; my energy is my compass.
48. I will always be gentle with myself regardless of what I face.
49. My feelings are valid, and I choose to honor them.
50. I breathe in love and breath out fears, self-doubts, and sadness.
51. I uproot everything that doesn't bring me joy.
52. I have everything because I have me.
53. I will rather blind the world with my beauty and intelligence than dim my light for someone else.
54. I am a chocolate-covered alien that doesn't need to fit neatly into any category.
55. I am okay with my uniqueness because it makes me who I am.
56. I have the right to choose what brings me love.
57. I am an amazing person.
58. I forgive myself for making mistakes.
59. My mistakes help me learn and grow.
60. I am okay just the way I am.
61. I am in charge of my happiness.
62. I have confidence and courage.
63. Today will be a great day.
64. Today I choose to think positively.
65. I can do anything.
66. I have everything I need.
67. I believe in my dreams and goals.
68. I have people around me who love and respect me.
69. I can make choices for myself.
70. I embrace my uniqueness and celebrate my unsettled mysteries.
71. I am a butterfly flying with bright, colorful, and powerful wings.
72. My wings are extraordinary and grow every time I am at ease.

73. The darkness of my cocoon is a space for metamorphosis.
74. I give myself grace as I help the world to fly.
75. I am happy when I start at the sun, eat healthy breakfasts, comb out my hair, and smile.
76. I choose to love myself and grow my wings.
77. I am aligned with my desires.
78. I manifest how things should be and not just how I want them to be.
79. I manifest what I want by being who I want.
80. I am connected with myself, and I know what it means to be loved by me.
81. I am committed to loving myself and pausing when things feel overwhelming.
82. My body makes me happy.
83. Loving myself unconditionally is a priceless gift I can give to myself.
84. I am capable of so much and more.
85. I believe in myself.
86. I deserve happiness.
87. Today, I choose to spread love.
88. I matter regardless of what others think.
89. My positive thoughts give me positive feelings.
90. I believe in myself.
91. Every day is a new day to love me.
92. I will only compare myself with myself.
93. Today will be my day.
94. I love my inner beauty and inner strength.
95. I am living in the moment.
96. I start my day with a positive mindset.
97. I will always accept who I am.
98. I am radiating positive energy.
99. Good and wonderful things will come to me.
100. I am the original version of myself; no fakers are allowed.
101. Today, I will shine.

102. I deserve everything good.
103. I choose to have an amazing day today.
104. I will continue working on myself to be the best version there is.
105. I am beautiful inside and out.
106. I am important and have a voice.
107. I am perfect just as I am.
108. I am in control of my happiness.
109. I choose my own attitude.
110. I am smart, and I accept myself just the way I am.
111. I have a beautiful imagination.
112. I see good in myself.
113. I am deserving of love and kindness.
114. I radiate compassion.
115. I am a strong source of power, and I can do anything.
116. I am peaceful, I am happy, and I am free.
117. I am loved no matter what.
118. Everything I need, I will receive.
119. I choose bravery today and every day.
120. I see all my awesomeness, and I appreciate it.
121. I love every part of me.
122. I release thoughts that don't serve me.
123. I shine like the sun.
124. I am grateful for all my body, mind, and spirit allowed me to do.
125. I am an endless rive of love.

CHAPTER TWO: AFFIRMATIONS FOR ENCOURAGING GROWTH

1. I will try out something new every day.
2. I release all resistance preventing me from expressing my creativity.
3. I learn every day from my experiences.
4. I am learning to be patient and strong.
5. I am strong and bold.
6. I have faith in myself.
7. I am constantly improving myself.
8. I am learning fast.
9. I am moving in the right direction.
10. I am using wisdom to navigate through life.
11. I am prepared for challenges.
12. I get wiser daily.
13. I draw conclusions from my experience.
14. My creative projects will satisfy me.
15. I feel good whenever I am creative.
16. I am exploring my unlimited potential.
17. I can create miracles in my life.
18. I can creatively express myself in any area I choose.
19. I am uniquely creative.

20. I am a wonderful black kid whose growth isn't stagnant.
21. People around me support my dreams.
22. I am happy with my growth.
23. I express myself with ease.
24. I am capable of doing great things.
25. I allow myself to be creatively fulfilled.
26. I am delighted by my creativity.
27. My skills and talents are appreciated by those around me.
28. My confidence will unlock doors for me.
29. I will reach all goals I have set for myself.
30. Once I can dream it, I can achieve it.
31. There are no goals out of my reach.
32. I am growing to be a strong kid for my parents.
33. I see growth in me.
34. I am better than I was yesterday.
35. I will keep improving with each passing day.
36. I see many growth opportunities.
37. I am patient because growth may take time.
38. My best self is about to emerge.
39. I am blessed all-around, and nothing will stop my shine.
40. I request what I need because I deserve everything good.
41. I am letting go of the things holding me back.
42. I am bidding negativity farewell.
43. Learning from my past mistakes is part of growth.
44. Nothing can deprive me of getting the things I want in life.
45. I am grateful for how far I have come.
46. I am thankful for the experiences that made me grow.
47. I won't allow fear to keep me from taking chances.
48. My comfort zone may not be my growth zone.
49. Experience is a good teacher; I am blessed for all the challenges I've faced.

50. I am responsible for the things in my life.
51. I know I can't change the past, but I will keep my focus on the future and make it bright.
52. I am walking out of my past constraints.
53. I am setting myself free by forgiving those who hurt me.
54. I am thankful for all the opportunities I've had to grow.
55. I am taking things one step at a time.
56. I will never remain stagnated.
57. I will surpass people's expectations because I know I am exceptional.
58. I will always seize my opportunities. I won't let them pass me by.
59. I am trusting myself to make the right choices.
60. My options are limitless; nothing can stop my progress.
61. I am confident in taking the first step toward a new goal.
62. I am focused on present results and future growth.
63. I am determined to achieve my life's dream.
64. I was born to excel.
65. I am a pacesetter.
66. I choose not to complain about the things I can't control. I choose to be strong.
67. I consciously work to bring the best out of every moment.
68. I am in charge of my reality; no one can define it for me.
69. I have a choice in every situation I find myself in.
70. I won't quit because it didn't work the first time.
71. I won't allow any obstacle to stand between men and my best self.
72. Today is promising, and I'm looking forward to what it holds for me.
73. I'm like a force of nature; I am unstoppable.

74. I won't be limited because of my race or color.
75. I am a living testimony of joy and happiness.
76. I will smile every single day because I can't be broken.
77. I won't make excuses to cover my mistakes. I will work harder to not repeat the same mistakes.
78. I am not afraid to express myself, a born leader.
79. One of my superpowers is that no one else can be me.
80. I am an intelligent being; I'm always evolving.
81. I am embracing everything about myself.
82. I learn from both the negative and positive sides of an event to help me make better decisions in the future.
83. Today is a good day to smile.
84. I choose to radiate love and inspire others to do the same.
85. I don't need the validation of someone before I live my best life.
86. I am whole and complete the way I am. I was made this way for a reason.
87. I know I was made to do big things, and I am embracing my full potential today.
88. I will no longer hesitate to allow people to see my light; I rather blind the world with my brilliance than hide my gifts.
89. Because my skin is a shade darker doesn't mean I can't lead, I am a leader.
90. People lacking alignment will fail to see how the universe supports my growth.
91. I may doubt myself and feel unsure at times, but knowing I was created for a purpose reminds me to keep on going.
92. A single tree can't become a forest; we all need each other to grow.
93. I see positivity, even in difficult situations.
94. I like trying new things, and that includes standing up for myself.

95. I am brave enough to ask for help.
96. I am courageous enough to ask questions.
97. Life is tough, but I am tougher.
98. Today is a good day.
99. I always strive to get better, not to become perfect.
100. I am a fast learner; I can learn new strategies to make things easier.
101. Good results require time and effort.
102. If I am struggling with something, it means I need more practice.
103. I am wired not to quit because I haven't tried the remaining one-hundred alternative ways I could have done it.
104. I am brave enough to chase after my dreams.
105. I won't know if I will reach my goals unless I try.
106. I may not like how things are today, but I can change the future.
107. Failing sometimes doesn't define me as a failure.
108. I am at the right place and at the right time because I am deeply loved.
109. I can do amazing things.
110. I am confident in myself and my abilities.
111. I can accomplish anything I set my mind to, and I'm willing to work for it.
112. I am stronger than any form of negative thoughts and procrastination.
113. Today is a good day to reward myself by learning something new.
114. I will start my day by being kind to someone.
115. I am excited to go to school and earn something new.
116. I am loved, cared for, protected, and safe.
117. I have a brilliant future waiting for me.
118. I am a natural winner.
119. I have a big heart; I engage in acts of kindness to help others grow.
120. There are so many exciting experiences out there just

waiting for me.

121. No matter what the outcome may look like, what matters is that I am growing and making progress.
122. I am just a kid; it's okay to ask for a hug when I'm feeling sad.
123. I am happy with who I am today.
124. I build habits that are helpful towards my success.
125. My imperfect actions are better than taking no action at all.

CHAPTER THREE: AFFIRMATIONS FOR SELF-ESTEEM AND CONFIDENCE

1. I learn every day from all that happens to me.
2. I'm learning to be patient, have faith, be strong, and be brave.
3. Life is my teacher, and I'm learning to cherish every moment of my life.
4. I am bold enough to be myself, and I don't need to be someone else.
5. If I respect myself, others will respect me.
6. I am wiser today and will keep getting wiser day by day as I learn new things.
7. I am worthy of recognition.
8. I'm confident in my color.
9. I am whole and complete.
10. Failures are new opportunities for me to grow.
11. I am comfortable in my skin.
12. Today, I'm embracing all there is about me.
13. I am special, and nothing can change that about me.
14. I celebrate my victories because I deserved them.
15. No one can write my story because I'm the author of my own life.

16. I am extraordinary and loved.
17. I love my hair type, the kinks and the curls are unique to my color.
18. I am sturdy because I'm black
19. My body is in the best shape it needs to be at this stage.
20. I'm beautiful, valuable, powerful, and I am black.
21. I'm whole and healthy.
22. I choose to feel good about myself.
23. I am at peace with who I am.
24. I love all of me.
25. I have a beautiful soul, and my appearance is a reflection of my soul.
26. I find my features wonderfully made.
27. I recognize that my imperfections as a sign of being human
28. I am in tune with my body and what it can do.
29. I was created to do amazing things.
30. I am at peace with myself and my environment.
31. I don't need to change anything because I am attractive as I am.
32. I love my colored skin; it has a unique feature that makes me who I am.
33. I know I am as beautiful as every other person.
34. I am fully responsible for my body; it must be loved, respected, and cared for.
35. I know my body's abilities and need to treat them well.
36. I am a natural leader.
37. I am confident, and people can see it in me wherever I go.
38. I will not bow my head in shame; I will smile all through the day.
39. I trust myself and the judgments I make.
40. I don't need to impress others because I know there is nothing to prove.

41. I know my self-worth, and I am holding my head up high.
42. People's opinions would no longer bother me.
43. My mental health means a lot to me.
44. I am kind.
45. I choose to love my world, and all is well within my world.
46. I can achieve anything I set my mind on.
47. I was created because the world needs me.
48. I am confident in the things I do.
49. My self-esteem is high because of my worth.
50. I am not dropping my standards for anyone.
51. I have the power to change things.
52. I am unstoppable.
53. I rise above low expectations and negative energy.
54. I am very proud of myself.
55. I embrace all that I am, and it fuels my confidence.
56. I'm in full control of my needs and desires.
57. I'm a pool of new ideas and perspectives.
58. My shortcomings aren't a result of my color and nor does it reflect on my race.
59. I might fail sometimes, but just like others, my failure doesn't define me.
60. The world isn't perfect, but I have decided to spread love still.
61. Instead of quitting, I will seek support to improve and push forward.
62. I am focused.
63. My goals are attainable.
64. I will surely reach my goals.
65. I'm filled with positive energy.
66. I'm excited to show the world what I can do.
67. I am ready to win.
68. I will be the best version of myself.
69. I'm not afraid of the unknown.
70. I can overcome any challenges that come my way.

71. I am in charge of my life, and I control my destiny.
72. I am confident in my potential and powers.
73. I am ready to stand out.
74. I know today will be a wonderful day.
75. I have high self-esteem.
76. Today, I will rise above my limits.
77. I'm a blessing to my peers and my generation.
78. I am worthy of good things, and I know so.
79. I am deserving of the love, care, and support I get.
80. I am deserving of the success I aim to achieve.
81. I choose to move forward with confidence.
82. I am a strong and confident brown skin human.
83. I will continue to conquer all the challenges I face.
84. I won't back away from challenges; they present a platform to prove my abilities.
85. I am here to be great.
86. I have a powerful presence; I won't be intimidated.
87. Happiness flows through and within me.
88. I am hard working.
89. I am capable of making smart choices.
90. I am grateful.
91. I can handle success.
92. I am growing.
93. I am a competent person.
94. My thoughts are creating new and great opportunities for me.
95. Everything I touch is a success.
96. I will meet new opportunities.
97. I am always receptive and open to learning new things.
98. I am allowed to dream and pursue my dreams.
99. I am determined.
100. I was born fully equipped with the things I need to succeed.
101. The world is my stage, and I am here to perform.
102. I will stand out from the crowd.

103. I will not be discouraged.
104. I possess the infinite potential to do great things.
105. I will no longer engage in poor habits.
106. I am respectful.
107. I will always complete my tasks.
108. I am like a sturdy black rock unmoved by the raging waves.
109. I am a go-getter.
110. I am unbothered by competitions.
111. I am a pacesetter
112. I am an asset with a high ability for success.
113. I am a great team player.
114. My color is never an excuse to fail.
115. I am impacting not only my life but others.
116. I am a valuable person in the world.
117. Today, I am inspired to work even harder.
118. I am willing to go the extra mile on my way to greatness.
119. Today, I will be taking one step further to reach my goals.
120. People recognize my worth and not my origins.
121. I am a problem solver.
122. I am open to constructive criticisms and will never stop improving myself
123. My goals are important; I won't be letting distractions get to me.
124. I am free.
125. I am human, and I'm progressing at the perfect pace.

CHAPTER FOUR: AFFIRMATIONS FOR MOTIVATION AND POSITIVE MINDSET

1. Look how far I've come; I am so proud of myself.
2. I am full of energy and joy that overflows.
3. I am building my future one step at a time with an unshakeable foundation.
4. I am infinitely talented, and I'll utilize them accordingly.
5. I won't allow negative thoughts to rule me; I am a happy soul.
6. I have a brilliant mind and a healthy body to achieve any goal I set.
7. From this moment, I choose to be confident in my abilities and happy with who I am.
8. Every new day is an opportunity for me to stay happy and positive.
9. Every new day is a blessing because I get the opportunity to spread love and positive vibes.
10. I feel strong, secure, and pumped, fully equipped to make my day great.
11. There's just a single me in this world, and I am not competing with anyone because I'm unique.

12. No matter the outcome, I'm satisfied with the knowledge that I'm growing and making progress.
13. I am an indispensable asset to the world.
14. With my talents and gifts, I will make everyone around me proud.
15. Good things come to me because I have a good heart.
16. I may make mistakes, but that's because I am human.
17. I will earn and grow resilient from my mistakes.
18. I have the right to express my feelings so that people can understand me.
19. I have all I need to become great and successful.
20. I won't be limited by what people say; I will grow into what I'm supposed to be.
21. I'm always proud of myself.
22. I will let compassion overcome any form of anger and hate.
23. The relationships I have with the people who love and care about me are an important part of my happiness.
24. I am blessed and guided by the universe toward the things I must learn and accomplish.
25. I am like a rose that thrives amidst thorns; nothing can stop and impede my growth.
26. I will always be good enough, smart enough, and strong enough to reach my goals.
27. I am thankful for all the things I have in life.
28. Today, I will only accept positive energy and vibes.
29. I am patient, calm, and in control of my emotions.
30. I'm starting today with a peaceful mind.
31. I am thankful for being filled with love, kindness, and peace of mind.
32. Every day is a new experience to learn, grow, and thrive.
33. I'm opening myself up for mind-blowing ideas to flow in.
34. I have the power to conquer the challenges and obstacles before me.

35. I have unlimited potential to be successful.
36. I choose to be happy.
37. I am letting go of any form of negativity standing between me and my peace of mind.
38. I am in total control of my mood, and my mental health is very important.
39. My life is very interesting, it's like an adventure, and I keep finding new and interesting things I can accomplish.
40. I am worthy.
41. I am in love with myself, my growth, and who I'm turning out to be.
42. I am passionate about life,
43. I am focused on the things that I need to do.
44. I am determined with an indomitable spirit.
45. I may be intimidated, discriminated against, or looked down on because of my skin. But I won't be deterred or broken from pursuing my dreams and reaching my goals.
46. I am a rare shade of brown; I'm amazing.
47. My thoughts are manifested into reality; I'm positive.
48. No matter how embarrassing a situation is, it will pass away, but I will be here because I am strong.
49. My opinions and thoughts are valid, and they matter.
50. I am thankful for every new day and grateful for this moment.
51. I am stronger and more resilient than I know.
52. I am colorfully motivated to overcome challenges and achieve goals.
53. I am a blessing to my community, and I will be an inspiration to future generations.
54. I have a healthy body, a healthy mind, and a healthy smile.
55. I am energized by the future I dream about.
56. I am accepting the mindset of hope, compassion, and optimism.

57. I will listen more than I speak.
58. I am capable of changing myself and improving where I lack.
59. I am challenging myself to grow.
60. Everything happens for a purpose, and it is for my ultimate good.
61. I don't care who is better than me because I am doing than I was yesterday. It's me against me.
62. I believe in myself, not the opinions of others.
63. I will never forget how powerful I am.
64. I know tough times are not forever. I am an indestructible powerhouse.
65. My future will be a result of what I do with my present.
66. I am intrinsically determined to be always happy.
67. I have decided to be compassionate and love unconditionally, regardless of people's actions toward me.
68. I am gold; the heat will only purify me.
69. I am ready to let the world know I am here.
70. I am a winner, and winners focus on winning.
71. I accept there is room for me to improve.
72. I will live an extraordinary life.
73. I will not be tied to my comfort zone by fear.
74. I am making my life for myself and striving to be the best version of myself.
75. I am safe and secure.
76. The world fills me with the warmth from the sunlight, and I am happy to be in a beautiful world.
77. I am not scared of the unknown.
78. Today is filled with so many possibilities.
79. I have faith in myself.
80. I trust my efforts, and I am ready to challenge the next phase of my life.
81. I am committed to accepting myself and my pace; I have nothing to prove.

82. I am open to infinite opportunities.
83. I am powerful and overflowing with positive energy.
84. I know life won't always be rosy, and things could get difficult before they become easy.
85. I am open to new ideas.
86. I won't allow what people say to get to me anymore.
87. I am ready to start my day with a smile.
88. Being a black kid is not a limitation.
89. I dwell in the light, setting myself free from all doubts and fears.
90. I choose to write my own story and create a world filled with love.
91. I won't beat myself up because of the things I can't control; I choose o focus on the things I can achieve.
92. I have choices. I choose to build and develop myself into someone who impacts society.
93. I am super excited because today presents a new opportunity for me to be useful.
94. I do not need to hide; the world needs me and the things I have to offer.
95. Nothing can limit me from fulfilling my life's purpose.
96. If I fall, I will always pick myself up and try again.
97. I have people that love, value, and respect me.
98. I can do better.
99. Today I choose to be confident and outspoken.
100. Anything is possible.
101. I am allowed to make mistakes; I am also allowed to learn and correct my mistakes.
102. I am prepared to make new exploits and achieve bigger things in my life.
103. I won't waste my precious time on hate, anger, sadness, or negative emotions.
104. I am fun to be with.
105. I know I have a beautiful soul and am not ashamed of myself.

106. Hello self, I'm super proud of you.
107. I only compare myself to the person I was yesterday.
108. I want to inspire other kids to love their dark skin just like I do.
109. I am like a pearl, surrounded by light.
110. I understand the value of my self-esteem, self-worth, and my limitless potential to grow.
111. I am willing to learn and improve myself in all the areas I find myself lacking.
112. I can overcome my challenges and succeed.
113. I am willing to take a chance.
114. I am smart, and I trust my decisions.
115. I have a great purpose on earth.
116. I won't apologize for being a happy person.
117. I trust my inner heart to guide me towards peace and happiness.
118. I am ready to take action.
119. I am grateful for the experiences I've had; they've thought me a lot.
120. I can do anything.
121. I am capable of handling responsibilities at my level.
122. All of my challenges have appropriate solutions.
123. There's no better time than now to make all the right choices.
124. I am an amazing person, and today will be my day.
125. I am blessed to have me.

FINAL WORDS

As parents or guardians, you can figure out how depressing and hurtful your kids would feel when bullied and discriminated against because of their skin color or race. Over time, they could begin to doubt the value of their existence, self-worth, and self-esteem.

These affirmations were carefully selected to help you draw out the good in your children, support them in building strong mental health, and create a positive buffer against negativity as they grow.

Always create uninterrupted time daily or weekly for your kids. Let them focus on you by looking into their eyes and confidently affirm them. Let them know they are loved. Let them know they are worth every single thing that is good in this world, and they fully deserve it.

Note that we all need mentors and positive role models to emulate. Let your kids talk about people they admire—the superheroes they love and would want to emulate. You can then point out the difficulties and challenges these people had to overcome to reach their goals. By pointing out these simple facts, your children will be able to relate to the affirmations they resonate with to grow their mindset and see failure as one of the things they would have to experience on their life's journey, and it's not something they should be ashamed of.

I want to leave you with one last affirmation, tell yourself, *"I am a great parent, and my kids are the best gifts the universe has given me."*

Best wishes!

Made in the USA
Coppell, TX
19 September 2022

83341069R00017